Cornerstones of Freedom

The Underground Railroad

R. Conrad Stein

CHILDREN'S PRESS®
A Division of Grolier Publishing
New York • London • Hong Kong • Sydney
Danbury, Connecticut

BY
HEWLETT & BRIGHT.

SALE OF

VALUABLE

SLAVES,

(On account of departure)

The Owner of the following named and valuable Slaves being on the eve of departure for Europe, will cause the same to be offered for sale, at the NEW EXCHANGE corner of St. Louis and Chartres streets, on *Saturday* May 16, at Twelve o'Clock, *viz.*

1. SARAH, a mulatress, aged 45 years, a good cook and accustomed to house work in general, is an excellent and faithful nurse for sick persons, and in every respect a first rate character.

2. DENNIS, her son, a mulatto, aged 24 years, a first rate cook and steward for a vessel, having been in that capacity for many years on board one of the Mobile packets; is strictly honest, temperate and a first rate subject.

3. CHOLE, a mulatress, aged 36 years, she is, without exception, one of the most competent servants in the country, a first rate washer and ironer, does up lace, a good cook, and for a bachelor who wishes a house-keeper she would be invaluable; she is also a good ladies' maid, having travelled to the North in that capacity.

4. [FANNY, her daughter, a] mulatress, aged 16 years, speaks French and English, [(having been in the North in that capac-] ity,) a good seamstress and ladies' maid, is smart, intelligent, and a first rate character.

5. [DANDRIDGE, a mulatto,] aged 26 years, a first rate dining-room servant, [and has] but few equals for honesty and sobriety.

6. [NANCY, his wife, aged] about 24 years, a confidential house servant, [good seamstress,] cook, washer and ironer, etc.

7. [MARY ANN, her child,] a creole, aged 7 years, speaks French and English.

8. [FANNY or FRANCES, a] mulatress, aged 22 years, is a first rate washer and ironer, good cook and house servant, and has an excellent character.

9. EMMA, an orphan, aged 10 or 11 years, speaks French and English, has been in the country 7 years, has been accustomed to waiting on table, sewing etc.; is intelligent and active.

Library of Congress Cataloging-in-Publication Data

Stein, R. Conrad.
   The underground railroad / by R. Conrad Stein.
       p. cm.— (Cornerstones of freedom)
   Includes index.
   Summary: Describes the operation, stations, and famous conductors of the underground railroad, a network that helped slaves escape from bondage prior to the Civil War in the United States.
   ISBN 0-516-20298-7 (lib.bdg.)   0-516-26140-1 (pbk.)
   1. Underground railroad—Juvenile literature. 2. Fugitive slaves—United States—History—19th century—Juvenile literature. [1. Underground railroad. 2. Fugitive slaves.] I. Title. II. Series.
E450.S835 1997
973.7`115—dc20
                                                      96-24122
                                                          CIP
                                                          AC

Harriet Tubman was told that she was born in 1820. She was never certain of her birth date because she was a slave, and the births and deaths of slaves were rarely recorded. As a child, Harriet worked in her master's kitchen. She often slept on the kitchen floor. Her food consisted of table scraps that she was forced to share with the master's dog. Whenever possible, however, Harriet defied the authority of her master. She once stood between a disobedient fellow slave and his furious master. The master threw a heavy piece of iron at the disobedient slave. Instead, the iron hit Harriet on the head, creating a terrible gash. As a result she developed epilepsy, a disease that can cause a person to fall asleep—without warning—at any time during the day or night.

In the slave-holding South, black children lived as slaves.

When she was twenty-nine years old, Harriet learned that she was going to be sold to another master, and she would be forced to leave her husband, brothers, and sisters. She decided to run away, even though she knew that escape was filled with danger. Harriet later recalled, "I had reasoned this out in my mind; there was one of two things I had a right to, liberty or death; if I could not have one [liberty], I would have the other [death]."

Slave auctions were common in the South, where white plantation owners bought and sold slaves.

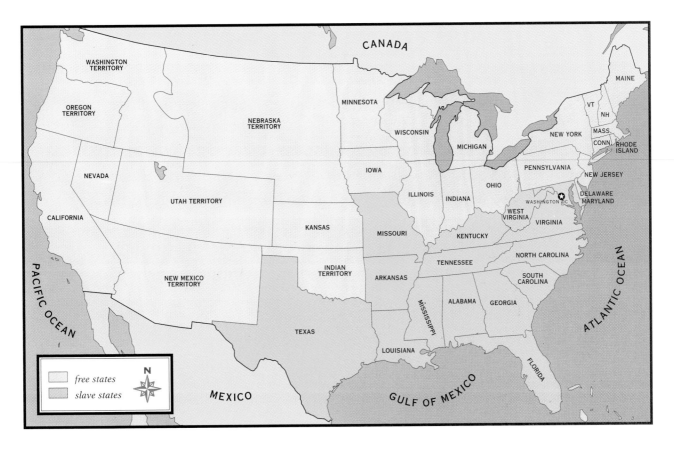

Map legend:
- free states
- slave states

N

One night in 1849, Harriet slipped out of the slave quarters of her master's Maryland plantation and began walking north. Harriet knew that if she looked for the North Star in the night sky and walked toward it, she would find her way to northern states, where slavery did not exist. Because she was black, she was forbidden by Maryland law from walking alone at night. She avoided roads, choosing instead to hike through wooded areas, where there was less chance of her being seen. Harriet knew that if she was caught trying to escape from her master, she would be returned to him and punished. But she continued her journey north, determined to reach freedom.

In the United States of the late 1850s, slavery was forbidden in the North, but was practiced in the South.

As she walked, she remembered a conversation she had several months earlier with a white woman who lived just a few miles north of the plantation where Harriet was a slave. The woman had said that she felt sorry for Harriet and that she wished there was something she could do to help her. Harriet wondered if the woman was one of the people who secretly broke the law in order to help slaves escape to freedom.

Harriet Tubman was twenty-nine years old when she escaped from slavery.

When escaped slaves found a stone marker such as this, they knew they had reached the Mason–Dixon line, which separated the North and the South.

Harriet knew where the woman lived and arrived safely. The woman welcomed Harriet inside and allowed her to rest. Then she gave Harriet some food and directed her toward another house where she could again find help and safety. From there, she was led to another house, and another, until she completed a 90-mile (145-kilometer) journey into Pennsylvania, a northern state where slavery was prohibited by law. "I looked at my hands to see if I was the same person," she said. "There was such a glory over everything. The sun came like gold through the trees."

Harriet Tubman had been escorted to freedom by the Underground Railroad, a secret network of courageous people who assisted escaped slaves by providing them with food and shelter. The Underground Railroad was such a well-kept secret that the origin of its name is uncertain. A story—which may only be a legend—tells of a slave named Tice Davids, who fled from his master's Kentucky farm in 1831. Davids ran toward the Ohio River. With his master in close pursuit, he began swimming to the opposite bank of the river. The slave owner followed in a rowboat, keeping a close eye on his runaway slave. On the far side of the river, Davids emerged in the slavery-hating town of Ripley, Ohio. A white man hid Davids in the basement of his house.

Davids's master walked the streets of Ripley for hours, searching in vain for the slave. When he finally gave up, the frustrated master said, "Davids must have gone off on some underground road." Thus, the term "underground railroad" was born. The organization was not an actual railroad, but the people involved in it used railroad terms. Railroads were new and thrilling conveyances whose tracks were just beginning to crisscross the United States. Houses where the slaves were hidden were called stations, the owners of the houses were called station-masters, guides were called conductors, and fugitive slaves were called passengers. In the years that followed her

escape to freedom, Harriet Tubman became a fearless conductor on the Railroad.

Blacks and whites worked together on the Underground Railroad. Because its members were breaking the law, the Railroad was loosely organized and had no single leader. Members of the Underground Railroad barely knew each other, but each of them shared a common goal— to abolish slavery in the United States.

Above: From the outside, houses that were stations on the Underground Railroad looked the same as any other house. Below: Railroad terms, borrowed from the country's newest form of transportation, were used to describe the Underground Railroad.

Slavery began in Jamestown, Virginia, the first permanent British colony in North America.

Black slavery began in the 1600s, when ships brought slaves from Africa to North America. During the 1700s, the United States was still just thirteen British colonies. As the War of Independence (1775–1783) approached, many Americans spoke out about the rights of all citizens. Those Americans believed that slavery did not belong in a country whose Declaration of Independence boldly proclaimed, "All men are created equal."

By the time the United States became an independent nation in 1783, slavery was already disappearing in the North. In the South, only a small number of whites owned slaves. Perhaps slavery would have faded in the South too, but an invention may have helped to extend its life. In 1793, a Massachusetts-born schoolteacher, Eli Whitney, built the cotton gin, a simple, hand-cranked device that separated the seed from cotton fiber. The machine made work previously done by hand much faster. Two years after the invention of the cotton gin, exports of cotton from the southern states increased forty-fold. The cotton industry, which required slave labor to pick the cotton crop, soon dominated the South.

Eli Whitney (left inset) invented the cotton gin (bottom inset) in 1793. In a few hours, the machine could do the same amount of work that fifty slaves could complete in a full day.

Most American slaves were terribly mistreated on their master's plantation. Often, fifteen or more slaves were crammed into dirt-floored cabins, some of which were no larger than a modern one-car garage. The dwellings were drafty in the winter and sweltering in the summer. Most adult slaves had chronic coughs and many suffered from frequent bouts of pneumonia and flu. Because of a poor diet, many slave children were infested with worms and had rotten teeth. Fewer than four of one hundred slaves lived to the age of sixty. A slave's workload was exhausting, and the punishments for not completing one's work could be brutal. To enforce discipline, some masters withheld food from slaves, whipped them, and bound them in chains. One slave owner said, "We teach

Slaves lived in cabins that were uncomfortable and overcrowded.

them that they are slaves [and] that to the white face belongs control."

Rebellions against slavery often began on the slave ships leaving Africa. African captives jumped overboard to escape a life of slavery. In North America, white southerners lived in fear of slave insurrections. A slave preacher named Nat Turner led a revolt in Virginia in 1831, in which sixty whites were killed. As a result of Nat Turner's rebellion, white southerners tightened laws restricting the lives of slaves. Many states passed laws forbidding whites from teaching slaves how to read. Other laws prohibited slaves from gathering together, except for Sunday church services. Even the services had to take place in the presence of a white preacher who made sure that no words of rebellion were uttered.

Nat Turner (second from left) was a slave and a preacher who led fellow slaves in a rebellion in Virginia in 1831.

Despite often difficult journeys, most fugitive slaves headed north, to states where slavery did not exist.

The restrictive laws only encouraged more slaves to escape. Some historians estimate that as many as 100,000 slaves fled from their masters between 1830 and 1860. Some escaped to the swamps and forests of Florida, where they joined the Seminole Indians. Others journeyed to Mexico. But the preferred route for an escaped slave was north. The escape routes were lined with stations on the Underground Railroad. Upon arriving in the North, a fugitive slave could easily blend into established communities of free blacks.

Because they operated in defiance of the law, members of the Underground Railroad had to keep their activities secret. Parents did not tell their children that they were giving refuge to runaway slaves because they feared that other children might find out and tell their parents. Townspeople and neighbors could collect large rewards by exposing Underground Railroad workers to the local sheriff. Children of station-masters sometimes heard soft knocks on the door of their homes late at night. Then they heard whispers, followed by a tense silence. Owners of houses on the Underground Railroad often devised clever hiding places for the fugitive slaves—removable floorboards, wagons with false bottoms, and woodsheds with concealed basements. Old barns and houses that still contain these hiding places have been preserved in several states, including Ohio, Pennsylvania, and Indiana.

Removable floor-boards in this barn led to a secret cellar where slaves rested until it was time to move on to the next station.

To the abolitionists (people who believed that slavery should be abolished), Underground Railroad workers were heroes. Southern slave owners, however, considered the workers to be thieves. Slaves were the property of their masters, and a strong slave could be worth as much as $2,000. Southern slave masters believed that anyone who helped escaped slaves was a criminal. Slave owners promoted false images of southern life where kindly masters ruled over contented slaves. Many owners said they could not understand why slaves wanted to escape from such good conditions.

Slaves worked from dawn to dusk on their masters' farms, but slave owners insisted the slaves were happy and well treated.

For the slaves, it seemed that the United States government firmly supported the slave owners. In 1850, Congress passed the Fugitive Slave

Law, which permitted an owner to hunt for an escaped slave anywhere in the United States. As a result of the law, slave owners hired people called slave catchers to hunt for runaway slaves. Black communities in the North lived in great fear of the slave catchers. Blacks responded by arming themselves against the slave catchers, or by encouraging escapees to move farther north to Canada.

Fugitive Slave Bill.

The Fugitive Slave Bill was passed into law in 1850. It gave slave owners the right to go anywhere in the United States to search for escaped slaves.

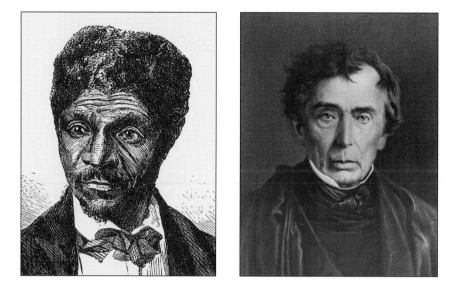

Dred Scott (right) and Chief Justice Roger Taney (far right)

In 1857, the Supreme Court issued the *Dred Scott* decision. Dred Scott was a slave whose master had once taken him to Illinois, a state where slavery was forbidden. Dred Scott sued his master for his freedom, arguing that a journey into free territory automatically made him a free man. Chief Justice Roger Taney of the U.S. Supreme Court disagreed with Dred Scott's argument. Taney claimed that when the U.S. Constitution was written, "the enslaved African race was not intended to be included [as citizens of the United States]." Therefore, as a noncitizen, Dred Scott was not eligible for the rights provided to other Americans by the Constitution.

The Fugitive Slave Law and the *Dred Scott* decision did not discourage slaves from escaping, however. Nor did these rulings discourage the work of the Underground Railroad.

The Levi Coffin house, one of the best-known stations on the Underground Railroad

Levi Coffin

Levi Coffin was perhaps the most famous stationmaster of the Underground Railroad. A white Quaker, he grew up in North Carolina. As a boy, he and his father witnessed a group of slaves forced to march over a road while chained to each other. The slaves were being taken to a market to be sold. Levi Coffin's father asked one of the slaves why they were chained. The slave replied, "They have taken us away from our wives and children and they chain us [in case] we should make our escape and go back to [our families]." Levi Coffin never forgot that awful sight. When he was only fourteen years old, he helped a slave escape from his master. As a grown man, Levi and his wife, Catherine, moved to southern Indiana, where they opened a country store. Over the course of many years, their house was a haven for hundreds of fugitive slaves.

In Delaware, Thomas Garrett's house was also a stationhouse on the Underground Railroad. During the years it operated, about 2,500 slaves were sheltered there. One of the slaves was Harriet Tubman. In the early days of the American Civil War (1861–1865), angry neighbors tried to attack Garrett because he was helping slaves, but Garrett was protected by free blacks who lived in a nearby community.

Another white stationmaster was Lyman Beecher of Cincinnati, Ohio. He was assisted in his work by his daughter, Harriet Beecher Stowe.

Harriet Beecher Stowe

In 1852, Harriet Beecher Stowe published a book called *Uncle Tom's Cabin.* The novel exposed the cruelties of slave life and dramatized the bravery of a black woman who escaped from her master with her baby. *Uncle Tom's Cabin* was such a controversial book that many Southerners were sent to prison for buying it, or even for having it in their homes. *Uncle Tom's Cabin* is still considered to be one of the causes of the Civil War.

Although whites put themselves in great danger by participating in the Underground Railroad, no one feared punishment more than the blacks who worked on the Railroad. Many of them were escaped slaves who faced re-enslavement if they were caught helping other fugitive slaves. Jermain Loguen was a runaway slave who served as a minister and as a

UNCLE TOM'S CABIN;

OR,

LIFE AMONG THE LOWLY.

BY

HARRIET BEECHER STOWE.

VOL. I.

ONE HUNDRED AND FIFTH THOUSAND.

BOSTON:
JOHN P. JEWETT & COMPANY
CLEVELAND, OHIO:
JEWETT, PROCTOR & WORTHINGTON.
1852.

Uncle Tom's Cabin, one of the most controversial books in U.S. history, exposed the harsh lives and terrible conditions that the slaves endured.

stationmaster. He wrote many anti-slavery sermons: "No day dawns for the slave. It is all night—night forever." Despite his fear of being returned to slavery, Loguen helped about 1,500 escaped slaves. He also founded schools for black children in New York.

William Still

William Still was a free black man who lived in Philadelphia, Pennsylvania. While working on the Underground Railroad, Still kept detailed notes. In 1871, Still's notes were published as a book called *Still's Underground Rail Road Notes*. It remains one of the most famous books describing the organization's work ever published.

One of the best-known of all the abolitionists during the 1850s was Frederick Douglass. Douglass was a runaway slave who operated a stationhouse from his print shop in Rochester, New York.

Some of the bravest workers on the Underground Railroad, however, were Southern slaves who assisted fellow slaves. On large plantations, the slave cabins were located almost completely out of sight of the master's house. The long distance allowed an escaped slave to sneak into another slave cabin for food and rest. Throughout the Southern states, slaves carried messages to each other. Spirituals, such as "When I'm Gone" and "Wade in the Water,

Frederick Douglass

Children," sung at church services and at prayer meetings, contained coded messages that told other slaves that a fugitive slave would soon be arriving at a station. The slaves also devised ways to warn each other of danger. If one lantern was hanging on the porch of a slave cabin, it was a sign to a fugitive slave that it was safe to enter the cabin. If two lanterns were hung on the porch, it was a warning to stay away until the danger passed.

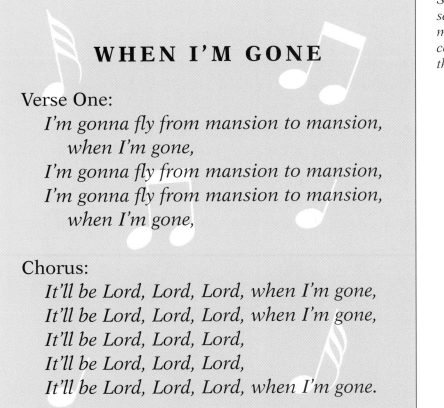

WHEN I'M GONE

Verse One:
    I'm gonna fly from mansion to mansion,
       when I'm gone,
    I'm gonna fly from mansion to mansion,
    I'm gonna fly from mansion to mansion,
       when I'm gone,

Chorus:
    It'll be Lord, Lord, Lord, when I'm gone,
    It'll be Lord, Lord, Lord, when I'm gone,
    It'll be Lord, Lord, Lord,
    It'll be Lord, Lord, Lord,
    It'll be Lord, Lord, Lord, when I'm gone.

Songs sung at church services and prayer meetings contained coded messages to the slaves.

Some slaves developed their own clever ways to escape from slavery without using the Underground Railroad. A slave couple from Georgia took a train north to Philadelphia—and freedom. The woman put on a man's top hat, wrapped her face in a bandage, and claimed that she was suffering from a toothache. She fooled the conductor into believing that her husband was a slave who was accompanying "him" to Philadelphia.

Henry "Box" Brown was sealed inside a crate and shipped from Richmond, Virginia, to Philadelphia's abolitionist headquarters. Not only did Henry "Box" Brown have to spend the trip hunched over inside a crate, but freight handlers also put the crate upside down. When the box was opened by abolitionists, "Box" Brown reportedly stood up and said with a smile, "How do you do, gentlemen?"

Henry "Box" Brown escaped from slavery by mailing himself from Richmond, Virginia, to abolitionist headquarters in Philadelphia, Pennsylvania.

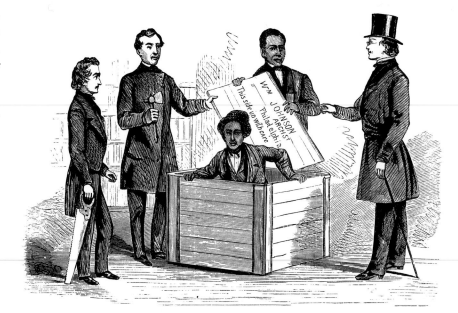

Many fugitive slaves were helped in their escapes by white Southerners who opposed slavery.

    Conductors on the Underground Railroad often journeyed south to help slaves escape from their masters. One of the most successful conductors was John Fairfield, a white man who was born into a slave-holding family in Virginia. As a boy, Fairfield befriended a slave child named Bill. When they were adults, Fairfield helped Bill escape. After that incident, John Fairfield became a conductor on the Underground Railroad, helping many other slaves to freedom. Southern slave owners considered Fairfield to be a Southerner because he grew up in Virginia. As a result, he often posed as a slave trader, which allowed him to travel freely with slaves through southern towns during daylight hours. Fairfield once took a group of twenty-eight slaves north to freedom by claiming he was taking them to a market to be sold.

In the years following her escape, Harriet Tubman traveled south eighteen times to rescue her family and three hundred other slaves.

The most celebrated of all conductors, though, was Harriet Tubman. After her escape at age twenty-nine, Harriet settled in Philadelphia where she scrubbed floors in a hotel. Using the money that she earned, Harriet journeyed back to Maryland to rescue her family. During the 1850s, Harriet made eighteen trips to the South and helped to free about three hundred slaves. She traveled only during the winter months, when the nights are longer than they are during the summertime. Harriet memorized the safest routes, which she used to take escaped slaves north. To disguise herself, she often dressed in men's clothing.

On several occasions, when Harriet feared they might be caught by slave catchers, she ordered the runaway slaves to march south. She reasoned that no slave catcher would believe that escaped slaves would travel in a southerly direction. She once hid a group of passengers under a pile of manure, giving them long straws to breathe through.

But Harriet's work was often hampered by her epilepsy. Without warning, she would doze off, sometimes sleeping for an hour or more. The escaped slaves under her protection could do little more than wait for her to wake up and continue the journey. Despite her disability, she constantly baffled southern slave owners, who offered a $40,000 reward for her capture. But the slaves considered Harriet to be like Moses of the Bible, who led the Hebrews out of slavery in Egypt. Today, Harriet Tubman is known as the "Moses of her people."

Harriet Tubman (far left) with slaves she helped to escape from the South

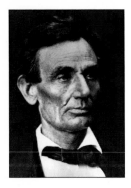

Abraham Lincoln

In the 1850s, the issue of slavery threw the United States into turmoil. In 1858, two years before Abraham Lincoln's presidential election, Lincoln declared, "a house divided against itself cannot stand. I believe this government cannot endure, permanently, half slave and half free." In 1861, Abraham Lincoln became president. One month later, South Carolina's Fort Sumter was fired upon, beginning the Civil War. In 1863, while the war still raged, President Lincoln issued the Emancipation Proclamation. It was the first step toward freeing the slaves. Then, in 1865, Congress ratified the 13th Amendment to the U.S. Constitution, which prohibited slavery in this country.

The Emancipation Proclamation, issued by President Lincoln in 1863, was the first step toward freeing the slaves.

But well before the war, thousands of blacks found their own freedom through the Underground Railroad. Alone or in small groups the slaves journeyed to freedom by following the North Star, just as Harriet Tubman did. The slaves used the handle of the Big Dipper as a guide to help them find the North Star. The slaves called the Big Dipper the "Drinking Gourd." A favorite song among passengers on the Underground Railroad contained the chorus:

Follow the drinking gourd.
Follow the drinking gourd.
For the old man is a-waiting for to carry you
*   to freedom.*
Follow the drinking gourd.

In this illustration from 1863, Freedom is depicted as a woman who forever removes the chains of slavery from the black race.

GLOSSARY

abolish – to put an end to

amendment – change or addition to a document

auction – sale where merchandise is sold to the person who offers the most money for it

conveyance – means of transporting an object

cotton gin – machine that separates the seeds from cotton

defy – to challenge authority

fugitive – person fleeing from the law

gash – long, deep cut

gourd – shell used as a drinking vessel

image – concept a person might have about a way of life that might be very different from reality

liberty – freedom

Mason–Dixon line – boundary line considered to be the border between the northern and the southern states

network – a system of things that are connected to each other

plantation – a large farm, which usually specializes in growing one specific crop

ratify – to approve or make valid

spirituals – type of religious songs developed mostly by southern slaves

fugitives

Mason–Dixon line

TIMELINE

1820 Harriet Tubman born

Nat Turner leads slave rebellion; The term "Underground Railroad" comes into use **1831**

Uncle Tom's Cabin published **1852**

1849 Harriet Tubman escapes from slavery

1850 Congress passes Fugitive Slave Law

1857

Dred Scott
decision

1860 Abraham Lincoln elected president

1861 Civil War begins

1863 Emancipation Proclamation issued

1865 Civil War ends; 13th Amendment ratified

1913 Harriet Tubman dies

INDEX (*Boldface* page numbers indicate illustrations.)

ABOUT THE AUTHOR
R. Conrad Stein was born and raised in Chicago, Illinois. After serving in the United States Marine Corp, he attended the University of Illinois, where he received a degree in history. He later studied in Mexico, then returned to Chicago and became a full-time writer. Mr. Stein is the author of more than eighty books, articles, and short stories for young readers. His most recent works for Children's Press include *The Assassination of Martin Luther King Jr., The Boston Tea Party, The Battle of the Little Bighorn,* and *Chuck Yeager Breaks the Sound Barrier.*